Gift

Gift

meditations from a spiritual journey

H. K. Stewart

The author can be contacted at the following:
    H. K. Stewart
    501.664.0500
    hks@hkstewart.com

ISBN: 978-0-9845341-1-1

Ask Press
P.O. Box 251301
Little Rock, AR 72225

Printed in the United States of America

This book is printed on archival-quality paper that meets
requirements of the American National Standard for
Information Sciences, Permanence of Paper, Printed
Library Materials, ANSI Z39.48-1984.

For Toni, Fran,
and Jackson

Contents

The tao that can be told is not the eternal
Tao. The name that can be named is not the
eternal Name.

—Tao te Ching, I

When all things began, the Word already
was. The Word dwelt with God, and what
God was, the Word was.

—John I:I

Ask. Seek. Knock.

Ask and you'll receive. Seek and you'll find. Knock and the door will burst open for you.

When Jesus made these claims, he wasn't talking about the material world of time and space. He was talking about our spiritual lives.

When we ask for spiritual insight, we receive it. When we seek spiritual truth, we find it all around us. When we knock on the door of the Tao, we discover there is no door.

What to Call It

God. Tao. Christ. Jehovah. Allah. Yahweh. Higher
Power. Gaia. Money. Sex-Drugs-and-Rock-and-Roll.

It doesn't matter what you call it. No word can point
to all of it. Since we find ourselves needing to talk
about it at times, though, we have to come up with
something we can use. Personally, I grew up calling
it God. These days, I don't know what to call it, so
I'll just call it The One.

In the beginning, there was The One and nothing
else. Now there's everything, and still just The One.

Every Red Is Different

Red flowers are red,
but a tulip is not a poppy,
and a poppy is not a rose.

Every instance of red is unique—
whether flower, bird, blood, or stone.
Why would we expect our spiritual paths
to be anything but one of a kind, too?

How Deep Is Deep?

Deep waters are deepest in mind
no matter how deep in reality.

No Claims

Sunlight reflects off the surface of a long river, and yet the river doesn't claim to be the sun.

Clouds drift across the face of a calm lake, and yet the lake doesn't claim to be the sky.

Gusts rattle the leaves of autumn trees, and yet the forest doesn't claim to be the wind.

The Divine shines on every spiritual path, so why would any path claim to be the only one?

The Five Pains

First is the pain we create for ourselves.
Second is the pain we create for others.
Third is the pain others create for us.
Fourth is the pain others create for themselves.

The first teaches humility.
The second teaches justice.
The third teaches forgiveness.
The fourth teaches compassion.

The fifth is the pain of not learning.
It teaches nothing.

Not Mine

My spouse's life is not mine.
My child's life is not mine.
My parent's life is not mine.
My sibling's life is not mine.
My friend's life is not mine.
My enemy's life is not mine.

When I let go of what is not mine,
I find I have everything I need.

Open Curtains

Light flows in when
curtains are open at noon.

Light flows out when
curtains are open at night.

It is as if your house is breathing.

Four Doors

When you are seeking a way out
of difficult circumstances, four doors
will forever open to your knock.

The first is the door of surrender.
The second is the door of defeat.
The third is the door of cleverness.
The fourth is the door of what is.

Forgiveness and Apology

Forgiveness is something I do in response to someone else's behavior.

Apology is something I do in response to my own behavior.

They are mirror images of one another—forgiveness and apology. They teach us both about ourselves and about others.

Another Farmer's Mare Story

I was shopping for a present several years ago when a thunderstorm rolled across the city. I was at an enclosed mall where the stores open onto a three-story atrium topped by a vaulted glass roof.

As the storm moved in, the sky grew dark, and the rains came down hard. For a time, I could hear hail hitting the glass. The noise was so loud that everybody around me stopped talking in mid-sentence and waited for the racket to pass. It was too loud to shout over.

I walked out to the atrium and looked up at the dark windows, then I looked down at the food court one floor below. I saw two young women sitting across from one another at a table, both animated and talking as if it were a bright and sunny day.

They were speaking in sign language, and they were the only people in the whole place who weren't drowned out by the storm.

Being Still

Stand still and calm the heart.
Sit still and calm the mind.
Lie still and calm the spirit.

Learning to be Patient

Learning to be patient when
you are not patient is hard.
Learning to be patient when
you are patient is easier.

Acts of God

Lightning strikes from ground and sky.
Tornadoes turn houses into missiles.
Hurricanes recast the boundaries of oceans.
Silence empties a space for the Divine.

Collecting Moments

To be aware and mindful and present in the moment
is difficult to carry off as the seconds of my life turn
into minutes and then hours and then decades.

When I can collect a moment here or there and
immerse myself in it as if sinking into a soothing
bath after a long day, that is almost enough to make
up for all of the moments I missed.

Almost enough.

What Separateness Brings

Separateness brings fear.
Fear brings suffering.
Suffering brings guilt.
Guilt brings pain.
Pain brings wisdom.
Wisdom brings compassion.
Compassion brings union.

Because Every Moment Is Unique

Because every moment is unique,
it contains a universe of possibilities.

Because every moment is unique,
it holds things you do not expect.

Because every moment is unique,
it requires your utmost attention.

Enlarging the Tribe

We are a tribal species. We build walls, set borders, and mark boundaries to set us apart from those who are not like us.

Sometimes we do this because we are afraid of those we do not understand.

Sometimes we do it because we must protect ourselves from those who would overrun us.

Sometimes we do it because we don't like how others live their lives or cook their food or raise their children or worship their god or make their music.

Sometimes we do it because we want things to go our way.

Sometimes we do it because we are addicted to the familiar.

Whatever the reason, it's important to remember that our true tribe is larger than we could ever imagine.

High Water

When a river overflows its banks,
it scours the landscape like a thief
and carries away what it does not own.

When my desires overflow my needs,
I become a river of selfishness
drowning any thought of others.

When my needs overflow my desires,
I become a dry valley with no memory
of how to go about praying for rain.

The Knock of Distractions

When a distraction presents itself at the gates of your mind, the interruption can be unwelcome.

At the same time, though, it pays to pay attention to that interrupting knock.

Sometimes, distractions are the only way insight can enter in.

Seven Mysteries

Mountains.
The ocean.
Birds.
Stars.
Journeys.
Newborns.
Wisdom.

Science and Spirituality

I can understand the battles between science and religion. They come from different points of view, and they have different goals.

To deny scientific discoveries because they conflict with a narrow reading of one sacred text or another is to place limits on our understanding of the Divine—and ourselves.

To separate science from the spiritual, however, is also a sad turn of events.

Moving the Boundaries

We push the boundaries of the universe whenever we try to see the edge of it.

We multiply the ten thousand things whenever we try to see the smallest thing.

For this reason, there is no edge, no smallest thing for us. There will always be more.

It is as if we bring the universe into being just by looking for it.

Not Every Adversary

Not every adversary is an enemy.
Not every loss is a defeat.
Not every mystery is a puzzle.
Not every question is a challenge.
Not every conflict is a battle.
Not every fear is a disaster.
Not every difficulty is a problem.

Study Hard

Innocence is our first teacher.
Curiosity is our second teacher.
Pain is our third teacher.
Wisdom is our diploma.

Go and See

What am I to do with my life?

Go and see.

The Bucket of Stars

One stormy afternoon, a man set out a bucket to catch rainwater, but when he checked it the next morning, it was almost dry.

How can this be? he thought. The rains beat on the roof all night long, so why is the bucket not full?

He picked it up and looked inside and saw dozens of tiny suns blazing in the bottom.

Look what the rains have left me, he thought.

He threw a blanket over the top and hid the bucket of stars in the pantry to save their light for the next rainy day.

Left or Right?

Inside the gate or outside the gate.
Which is more useful?

In the sunlight or in the shade.
Which is more natural?

In the valley or on the peak.
Which is more vigorous?

Open hand or closed hand.
Which is more wise?

The Simple Life

As I grow older, it becomes easier to see the bones of my life. I come to realize how simple it all is.

My needs become stripped down like winter trees. My grievances turn into dry twigs. And every moment is filled to overflowing if I will only open my eyes.

Gifts of Growing Older

What is wisdom?
The answer to the question
before the question arises.

What is insight?
The discovery of a truth inside
that is also mirrored outside.

What is vision?
The recognition of one's path
as it becomes one's path.

The Pearls of Pain

All pain, no matter where it comes from, contains within it a pearl of great value. The greater the pain, the more precious the pearl.

However, we must believe the pearl is indeed in our pain, and we must look for it. Otherwise, we'll never gain its benefit, and our suffering will become a gift we never unwrap.

Breathing on My Own

Only I can breathe my own breath.
Only I can hear my own blood in my ears.
Only I can step in my own footprints.
Only I can live in fear inside my own skin.

When I let go of breathing and blood,
I let go of the fear of their absence.
When I let go of footprints and skin,
I let go of the fear of being alone.

Burn

Tragedy generates its own heat,
burns away the chaff of our lives,
and clears the way to higher ground.

Stop Worrying About Your Name

We cannot control what other people think of us.
We can try to influence what they think by the way
we treat them, but we don't get to decide how they
actually see us.

We can only control what *we* think of ourselves.
And the only true way we can control what we
think of ourselves is to become who we want to
think we are.

To become who we want to think we are, we start by
discovering who we are. We do this by looking back
at ourselves—to see ourselves as another might.

This is how the universe begins.

Three Awarenesses

The first awareness is
to clear out spaces for the divine.

The second awareness is
to accept the unchangeable.

The third awareness is
to discover we are all divine.

Helping the World

If you want to help the world become a better place, don't start with the whole world. It's too big.

It's much easier to help one person have a better life. In helping that one, you help the whole world.

The Split in the Woods

I follow a path into the woods.
The path gets narrower, overgrown.
The woods grow darker the farther I go.

Then suddenly, the path splits.
One to the left. One to the right.
I look at the two paths and where
they each seem to be heading.
I think about where I am in the world
and calculate where each path
might eventually take me.

Then I look down each one
as far as I can see,
and then I make a choice.

Then I ask myself,
did I make a choice?
Or did the choice make me?

Letting Go of Who I Am

When I let go of who I am,
I allow myself to come into being.

Rituals

Rituals are one of the ways we mark our individual and collective journeys through life. They give us little set-pieces we can trust to be the same (more or less) each time we go through them.

They also help us connect to one another, both as individuals and as a community. When we celebrate a friend's birthday, we're also celebrating our own birthdays. When we celebrate a national holiday, we're also reconnecting ourselves as a national community.

Rituals show us where we are at a given time and place. Knowing where we are helps us know what step to take next.

A Summer That Might Have Been

One spring, the new leaves on every tree came out in brilliant fall colors—from pale yellow to deep orange to blood purple.

Everyone in town wondered what it could mean. Some said it was a sign from heaven. Some said it was a sign of impending doom. Some explained it scientifically.

As spring gave way to summer, the leaves darkened into a deep green that grew lighter as the summer wore on. By the time the leaves dropped off in the fall, they were all a bright and vital green, as if they'd just unfurled in a normal spring.

That was years ago, and now, no one can prove it happened or it didn't happen.

But everybody has an opinion.

To Be Grateful

To be grateful for an escape is natural.
To be grateful for a gift is courteous.
To be grateful for a painful day is wise.

Winter Solstice

On the shortest day of the year,
the sun sits motionless on the lip of winter.
A new season begins as another year ends.
The universe continues its unfolding
like an endless bolt of cloth.
To ask why is useless, but
it's still a worthwhile meditation
on such a long, clear night.

Between Storms

Rain falls staccato
on a flooded storm drain.

Runoff rushes down the curb
like wind along a ski run.

Pools disappear into the pores
of beige naked ground.

Iron clouds dry out
and turn aluminum gray.

And once again,
we find ourselves
between storms.

Pilgrimage

Every step we take is a pilgrimage—because every step we take is a step along the journey we make every day across our own holy ground.

Discernment and Faith

Discernment comes when we reach a crossroads that isn't on our map—when there's no clear way forward. When we can't get the answers we need from outside ourselves, we have to turn to the only other place available to us—inside.

This is discernment. Its fruits are the answers that grow within us when we seek insight.

But where do the answers come from? How do we know we can trust them?

We don't. This is why we invented faith.

Blink

We blink to soothe our eyes.
We swallow to wet our throat.
We breathe to fill our lungs.

How do we blink to soothe our conscience?
How do we swallow to wet our passion?
How do we breathe to fill our soul?

Community Project

When I am one, I know myself one way. When we are more than one, we begin to know ourselves in more than one way.

Learning myself is my life's work. Learning who I am also means learning who I am not.

Communities help me do this by showing me different points of view of who I am.

Wherever two or more are gathered together, a community is born.

We are all community projects.

Questioning Enemies

What is the value of having an enemy?
How does an enemy help us know who we are?
What can an enemy teach us that no one else can?
Who gets to decide who our enemy is?
When does an enemy stop being an enemy?
Who gets to decide that?

The Gift of Gratitude

To feel grateful for what you have is itself a gift to be thankful for. Gratitude is its own reward.

There Are Many Paths

There are many paths
to the same destination.

Some are direct.
Some are dangerous.
Some are wandering.
Some are wayward.
Some are clearly marked.
Some are newly blazed.
Some are overgrown.
Some have not been made yet.

When I See My Connectedness

When I see my connectedness,
I recognize my oneness.

When I see my oneness,
I recognize my divinity.

When I see my divinity,
I recognize my abundance.

When I see my abundance,
I realize salvation is already mine.

Listening to Judgments

Believing I am not good enough is not the same as believing I am not acceptable.

When I believe I am not good enough, I am listening to judgments from within.

When I believe I am not acceptable, I am listening to judgments from without.

When I learn to believe I am good enough, I am listening to the way things really are.

Feeding the Hungry

When we feed the hungry among us, we are also feeding the Tao. When we feed the Tao, we are also feeding ourselves.

All are one in the Tao.

When we clothe the ragged, comfort the sick, or visit the imprisoned, we are also attending to the Tao. When we attend to the Tao, we are also attending to ourselves.

All are one in the Tao.

How do we know this? By how we feel when we feed, clothe, comfort, and attend to others.

And by how we feel when we don't.

Five Spices

Help somebody.

Be grateful.

Pay attention.

Be intentional.

Care as much as you can.

If I Ask a Sign

If I ask a sign of the Tao,
and the Tao gives me a sign,
how do I decide whether to believe
it is indeed a sign from the Tao
or my own wishful imagination?

I cannot know
which is true.
I can only choose
which to believe is true.
My best choice is
to believe I shall see clearly.

First, I Must Accept

First, I must accept
I have something to see,
then I can see it.

First, I must accept
I have something to hear,
then I can hear it.

First, I must accept
I have my own path,
then I can find it.

First, I must accept
I have my own way,
then I can follow it.

Talking to the Divine

Can I talk to the Divine?
Of course.

Will it listen?
Of course.

Will it respond?
Of course.

Will I know this?
Only if I am willing to know.

Reflections

Open the door to the world beyond yourself, and you will see yourself reflected in its many surfaces.

When you look below the surface, you realize you have been there all along—and all the universe with you.

The Bending Tree

The tree that bends withstands the storm.
The reed that bends withstands the river.
The dancer who bends withstands the dance.

A bending flash burns away forests.
A bending river wears away stone.
A bending soul wears away adversity.

Letting Go

When you let go of controlling the world,
the door of your cell swings open before you.

Opinions

Opinions help us make decisions.

Decisions help us take action.

Taking action helps us move.

But move toward what?

We move toward peace and justice when our actions are guided by compassion.

We act in confidence when our decisions are grounded in wisdom.

We make better choices when our opinions are based on direct experience.

Four Things

Four things bind us together.

The birth of a child.
A common enemy.
The setting sun.
The fear of being alone.

Four things separate us.

Belief in only one way.
Infallible scriptures.
The fear of dying.
God's exploration of discreteness.

Crossing a Stream

When crossing a stream from rock to rock, it is not always easy to tell which stones are solid and which ones will topple underfoot.

Best to step lightly.

Four Houses

The first is the dwelling of the powerless.
The second is the dwelling of the determined.
The third is the dwelling of the selfish.
The fourth is the dwelling of the tolerant.

When you enter the first, be full of respect.
When you enter the second, be full of questions.
When you enter the third, be full of praise.
When you enter the fourth, be full of thanks.

Dust on Dust

I arose from dust
and I will return to dust.
How many ancestors
carry me forward
step by step every day,
masquerading as the earth
under my feet?

The Perfect Illusion

Maybe perfection is an illusion.

How can anything be perfect
when everything is different?

How can anyone be perfect
when everyone is one of a kind?

How can one moment be perfect
when every moment is unique?

If perfection exists, how can it be
anything but what already is?

Three Paths

We each follow
three paths in our lifetime.

The first is the path
of our parents and ancestors.
This is the way things were.

The second is the path
of our friends and peers.
This is the way things are.

The third is the path
of our children and grandchildren.
This is the way we want things to be.

Reflections of a Spiritual Life

Our religious life reflects our spiritual life.

When our spiritual life is sick, our religious life is full of fear, and our actions betray it.

We become judgmental, arrogant, intolerant. We condemn. We demonize. We exclude.

When our spiritual life is well, our religious life is patient and giving and kind.

We become compassionate, accepting, complete. We contemplate. We discern. We build community.

God in a Box

I don't know what to call it. All I know is that I came from it. I move and breathe and have my very being in it. I'll return to it when I die.

I'm good with that.

Is it God? Is it the Tao? Is it Allah? Is it Gaia? Is it Sex, Drugs, and Rock and Roll?

No.

No box is big enough.

Decades in the Wilderness

The distance from one point along our spiritual journey to another may look short, but it can take decades of wandering in the wilderness to travel the space between them.

The reason is because it can take decades for our original ideas about the journey to die off, one by one.

No way into the promised land before then.

Sometimes It Is Easier

Sometimes it is easier to hear
in the middle of noise than it is
to hear in the middle of silence.

Sometimes it is easier to see
in the middle of darkness than it is
to see in the middle of light.

Sometimes it is easier to believe
in the middle of chaos than it is
to believe in the middle of church.

Sometimes it is easier to live
in the middle of dying than it is
to live in the middle of life.

Following a Stray Dog

A man was following a stray dog down the street
one morning when a friend saw him and called out.

"What are you doing?" the friend asked.

"I'm following this stray dog," the man answered.

"Why?" the friend called.

"It is my job today."

"To follow a stray dog?" the friend asked.

"No, to see where he is going."

Travel Guide

When the way is clear,
we move forward at a steady pace.

When the clouds move in,
we go more slowly.

When the fog is too thick to see the path,
we slow to a crawl.

When darkness is upon us,
we sit and wait.

Act on what you know.
Wait for what you don't know.

Shifting Borders

One candle can light a dark room. It covers every object with shadows and light. Some surfaces lit; some surfaces dark.

What gives shape to everything, though, is not the light or the dark, but rather the shifting border between the two.

This is where depth begins.

The Snake and the Mouse

The snake said to the mouse one morning in the corner of the field, "You have eaten well, my friend. You're quite a tasty morsel."

"Gout," answered the mouse. "It's a misery to live so high."

"Then let me dispose of your misery for you, sir," said the snake.

"Oh, but I would be gone with it, and you would inherit a terrible pain in your tail. I'm not worth the trouble," the mouse replied as he slowly turned and waddled away.

The snake flicked his tongue and followed not far behind.

Small Things

Large follows small.

What we do in a small way,
we will do in a large way.

Another reason to pay
attention to small things.

Try Not to Mistake

Try not to mistake fear for laziness.
Try not to mistake shyness for arrogance.
Try not to mistake modesty for ignorance.
Try not to mistake humility for weakness.
Try not to mistake compassion for innocence.

Making Ripples

Every pebble on the shore of a lake holds within it
an infinite supply of ripples.

This is where you come in.

Do Birds Know?

Do birds know I am listening to them sing?

Do trees know I am cooling myself in their shade?

Do flowers know I am sniffing their fragrance?

Does the sun know I am warmed by its light?

Does the earth know I am on my way there?

A Bell Rings Once

A bell rings once
in the distance.

A church bell?
A temple bell?
A clock bell?
A dinner bell?
An alarm bell?

How can we tell
from just one clap?

For those who know its sound,
one note is enough.

That and listening.

When a Question Arises

When you go looking for an answer to some question that keeps pushing its way into your mind, how can you be sure the answer isn't secretly begging you to find it?

How do you know the question that keeps plaguing you didn't originate with the answer you're trying to find?

What if the mystery you keep trying to solve is really just the solution trying to attract your attention?

How do you know that questions rising in your mind aren't really answers shouting to you at the top of their lungs?

Liking My Neighbor

Do I have to like my neighbor? No.
Do I have to love my neighbor? Yes.

How can that be?

To like your neighbor is to enjoy your time with her.

To love your neighbor is to recognize her as another
part of the wholeness we all are—regardless of
whether you like her or can't stand her.

The Mystery of Life

What a mystery it is to be alive.

What a terror, a blessing, a dream, a curiosity it is to wake up each morning and realize we're still in the world.

What a painful joy. What an amusing bewilderment. What a brilliant darkness, an opaque light.

No wonder we keep showing up for it.

When Do I Not Have Time?

Do I have time for this moment?
Do I have time for this task at hand?

When do I not have time for this moment?
When do I not have time for this task at hand?

The Longer Journey

I can walk back and forth
to my neighbor's house
day after day after day and see
something new every time I go.

I can also travel around the world
and never really notice anything
and in the end come back home
empty-headed.

Which is the longer journey?

A Great Circle

We are each a great circle.
When we travel out of ourselves
along that arc, we discover
a universe that just keeps unrolling.
When we journey along that arc
into ourselves, we discover
the same universe within.
When we discover the universe,
whether within or without,
we realize how much more
there must be.

When You Look

When you look,
the tulip will bloom.

When you listen,
thunder will rattle the windows.

When you taste,
the ocean will turn salty.

When you sniff,
the wind will smell like rain.

When you touch,
marble will turn cool.

The universe is waiting
for you to pay attention.

Turning Point

The earth turns into plants
then into animals and then
back into dirt once again.

The ocean evaporates
into clouds then turns into rain
then into streams and rivers
then into the ocean again.

See? Every turn is
another starting point.

The Path Before You

Your path will find you. It will lay footprints under your feet.

Pay attention to what comes before you and take the next step.

Balancing Act

Courtesy balances tolerance.
When someone is tolerant toward me,
I should be courteous in return.

Humility balances adoration.
When someone showers me with praise,
I should remember how small I really am.

Gratitude balances kindness.
When someone treats me with kindness,
I should fully appreciate the gesture.

Generosity balances attention.
When others offer me their attention,
I should give them the best I have to offer.

When the Teacher Is Ready

When the student is ready, the teacher will appear.

This is true.

It is also true that when the teacher is ready, the student will appear.

A good student is the secret to good teaching.

Five Mountains

One mountain is for climbing.
It is the one in front of you.

One mountain is for distance.
It is the one you are standing on.

One mountain is for silence.
It is the one you are deep within.

One mountain is for questioning.
It is the one you will never reach.

One mountain is for rest.
It is the one you know like the back of your hand.

Enemies Under the Same Roof

If a man finds he has enemies in his own house, it is more likely he invited them in himself than that they broke in against his will.

We help to create what we oppose.

When I Am on My Path

When I am on my path,
the way is smooth and clear,
the air sunny and warm.

When I am on my path,
the difficult becomes simple.
Answers arrive before questions.

When I am on my path,
everything I need shows up
when I need it, right on cue.